THE SUMMER OLYMPICS

by Caroline Arnold

An Easy-Read
Sports Book
FRANKLIN WATTS 1983

A GROLIER COMPANY

New York | London
Toronto | Sydney

FOR MY BROTHER
TOM

Cover photograph courtesy of
United Press International

Photographs courtesy of: United Press International: pp.
4, 8, 11, 12, 14, 15, 16, 17, 18 (both), 21 (both), 25 (both),
26, 27, 28, 29, 30, 31, 38, 40, 41, 43, 44, 45, 46; New York
Public Library Picture Collection: p. 7; Wide World Photos:
pp. 22, 33, 34, 42; Sygma (Habans): p. 37.

Library of Congress Cataloging in Publication Data

Arnold, Caroline.
The Summer Olympics.

(An Easy-read sports book)
Includes index.
Summary: Briefly discusses the origin of the
Olympic games, who organizes the games today, and
the eight events that make up the summer games.
1. Olympic games—Juvenile literature.
(1. Olympic games) I. Title. II. Series.
GV721.5.A855 1983   796.4'8   83-3672
ISBN 0-531-04622-2

R.L. 3.0 Spache Revised Formula

Contents

The First Olympic Games

Every four years athletes from all over the world meet together at the Olympic games. There they compete against each other in sports. The winners take home medals and diplomas. They are proud because they are the best amateur athletes in the world in their sports.

Nearly 3,000 years ago athletes in ancient Greece competed in much the same way. They met on a broad, flat plain called Olympus. Athletes came from all over Greece to race, jump, and throw. These ancient Olympic games were so important that wars would stop so they could be held.

Montreal, 1976:
Runners carry the torch
into Olympic Stadium.

Today the site of the ancient Olympic games is in ruins. But we remember it with a special torch. That torch is lit in Greece. Then runners carry it to the place where the Olympics will be held. There it burns brightly during the games.

The first modern Olympic games were held in the summer of 1896 in Athens, Greece. They were started by a Frenchman named Pierre Coubertin. He wanted more sports competitions for athletes. He also thought that this was a good way for people from different countries to meet together peacefully.

Since 1896 the Olympics have been held every four years except when there were world wars. Each four-year period is called an Olympiad. The 1896 Olympics was the first Olympiad. This means that the 1984 Olympics is the twenty-third Olympiad.

Winter sports were added to the Olympics in 1924. The 1984 Winter Games are the fourteenth Winter Olympics.

Cities all over the world take turns hosting the Olympic games. Before television was invented, you could only see the Olympics if you went to the place where they were being held. Today most people watch the events at home.

Athens, 1896:
The first modern Olympic Games

*Montreal, 1976: Canadians form
the five-ring Olympic symbol.*

Who Organizes the Olympics

The Olympic games are organized by a group of people called the International Olympic Committee. It chooses the events and makes the rules. Each sport must be played in at least twenty-five countries. Also, at least twelve countries must enter the Olympic competition. A sport may be played just as a demonstration and not for prizes. Baseball is sometimes a demonstration sport.

Most sports have both men's and women's events. It would not be fair for men and women to compete against each other in most sports. Many sports have different rules and different equipment for men and women.

Only amateur athletes may compete in the Olympics. An athlete is an amateur if he or she is not paid to perform. Each athlete must also be a citizen of the country he or she represents.

Each country in the world may have at least one person in each event. Different countries choose their athletes in different ways. In the United States a group called the United States Olympic Committee chooses athletes for the Olympics. They try to choose the best people that they can.

In every Olympic event there are prizes for the winners. Sometimes the winner is the fastest. Sometimes the winner goes the farthest or highest. Sometimes the winner has scored the most points. Sometimes the winner is judged to be the best. Each sport has its own rules for winning.

The first six winners in each event get diplomas. The first three prize winners also get medals: gold for first, silver for second, and bronze for third. Prizes can only be won by teams or individuals. Countries cannot win prizes at the Olympics. However, a country is proud when members of its Olympic team bring home lots of medals.

Munich, 1972:
Swimmer Mark Spitz
(U.S.) accepts
a gold medal.

Montreal, 1976: Over 9,000 athletes crowd the field during opening ceremonies.

The Summer Games

In the first modern Olympics there were 285 people from 13 countries. Now more than 10,000 athletes take part in just the Summer Olympics. They come from 151 countries and participate in many events in 22 different sports.

TRACK AND FIELD

One of the most popular Olympic sports is track and field. Track events include all kinds of footraces. They may be short races called sprints or dashes. Or they may be long races that last a mile or more. The races are usually held on an oval racetrack.

Field events are for throwing and jumping. They are usually held on a flat field. Often this is in the center of a race track.

Running Events

Most races at the Olympics are measured by the metric system. The 100 meter (328-foot) dash is the shortest race. In a dash or sprint the runner runs full speed to the end. The first runner to touch the tape at the finish line is the winner. In a long race the runner begins slowly and then speeds up at the end. The runner does not want to run out of energy before the race is over.

Opposite: Montreal, 1976: Runners from all over the world compete in the 100-meter race. Left: Munich, 1972: Frank Shorter (U.S.) wins the marathon.

The longest race in the Olympics that one person can run is the marathon (26 miles, 385 yards). For a long race the runner may go around the track many times. Or the race may be run through a park or the countryside. Then it is called a cross-country race.

The only other race that is not measured in meters is the 1-mile (1.6-km) race. For many years no one was able to run the mile in less than four minutes. People believed that it could not be done. Then in 1954 an Englishman, Roger Bannister, beat the record. He ran the mile in 3 minutes and 59.4 seconds. Since then many people have run the mile even faster than that.

The racetrack is divided into lanes. Each runner starts in his or her own lane. The runners in the outside lanes start farther forward than the runners in the inside lanes. This may look as if they get a head start. But they don't. They need to start ahead because the outside lanes are longer than the inside lanes. Runners may change lanes if they pass each other.

Sometimes during a race runners jump over ten small fences. They are called hurdles. Low hurdles are 2½ feet (.75 m) high. High hurdles are either 3 or 3½ feet (.914 or 1.1 m) high. In the steeplechase race the runners must jump over hurdles, low bushes, and pools of water.

In a relay race there are four runners to a team. Each member of the team runs one fourth of the race. The first runner carries a small wooden or metal stick called a baton. Each runner passes the baton to the next runner on the team. The fastest runner on the relay team always runs last.

In a walking race the people walk very fast. Their hips move up and down and their arms swing. With each step the heel must touch the ground first. It is hard to walk fast. At that speed it would be easier to run.

Munich, 1972: A walking race begins.

Left: Munich, 1972: East Germany's Wolfgang
Nordwig clears the bar at 5.5 meters.
Right: Munich, 1972: Randy Williams (U.S.)
takes the long jump in stride.

Jumping Events

The jumping events at the Olympics test who can jump the highest and who can jump the farthest. In all the events there is a pit filled with soft material for the jumpers to land on. This way no one gets hurt.

In the high jump a bar is placed across ledges on two posts in the ground. The bar falls off easily if it is bumped. Each person has a turn to jump over the bar. Anyone who knocks the bar down is out of the competition. After everyone has had a turn the bar is raised. People have jumped over 7 feet (2.1 m) in the high-jump event.

The pole vault is like the high jump except that the bar is much higher. Each person uses a long pole to boost himself up and over the bar. Men have jumped over 18 feet (5.3 m) in the pole vault. Women do not compete in this event.

In the long jump each person runs a short distance to a takeoff board. The runner then jumps forward as far as he or she can. It is important to fall forward after landing. The judges measure the distance from the board to the nearest point where the person touched the ground. In the triple jump the runner first hops, then skips, and then jumps.

Throwing Events

In four events at the Olympics athletes test their skill at throwing. In the shot-put event each person heaves a heavy iron ball as far as possible. The ball is called a shot. It is so heavy that it cannot be thrown like a ball. Instead it must be pushed away from the body. It is like trying to throw a big rock.

In the discus throw athletes hurl a wooden disk into the air. The disk is something like a solid Frisbee made of wood. It is heavier than a Frisbee. But like a Frisbee it can be thrown hundreds of feet.

The javelin throw is a modern version of ancient spear-throwing contests. The javelin is a long spear made of wood or metal. Each person runs for about 100 feet (30 m) and then throws the javelin into the air. World records for the javelin throw are over 300 feet (90 m). That is longer than a football field!

The only throwing event that is just for men is the hammer throw. The "hammer" is a 16-pound (6.8-kg) metal ball with a handle made of wire rope. Each man holds the handle and swings the ball around and around. Then he lets go and throws it as far as he can. The world's record for the hammer throw is more than 250 feet (77 m).

Left: Munich, 1972: Deborah van Kiekebelt (Canada) rears back to hurl the shot. Right: Munich, 1972: Ludvik Danek of Czechoslovakia makes a gold-medal winning discus throw.

Decathlon

The decathlon is a group of ten events in track and field. It is a test of overall athletic skill. Each person must be able to do the 100 meter (110-yard) dash, long jump, shot put, high jump, 400 meter (440-yard) run, 110 meter (120-yard) high hurdles, discus throw, pole vault, javelin throw, and 1,500 meter (1,560-yard) run. Many athletes are good runners, good jumpers, or good throwers. But it is hard to be good at everything.

It is possible to earn 1,000 points in each event in the decathlon. If a person won every event, he or she would earn 10,000 points. An Olympic record for the decathlon was set in 1976 by Bruce Jenner from the United States. He earned 8,618 points!

An easier version of the decathlon is the pentathlon. It has only five events.

Montreal, 1976:
Bruce Jenner
(U.S.) crosses
the finish line.

WATER SPORTS

Swimming and Diving

Just as in footraces, swimming races are held for both short and long distances. Usually, the swimmer must use just one kind of stroke in each race. It may be the crawl, the breaststroke, butterfly stroke, or the backstroke. In the freestyle races swimmers always use the crawl because it is the fastest. The medley race uses a combination of all the strokes. Swimmers also do relay races.

In diving competitions swimmers jump off diving boards high above the water. While in the air they do acrobatic turns and twists. In many ways diving is like gymnastics. Each move must be perfectly timed. Diving competitions are scored by points. The diver with the most points wins.

Synchronized swimming is a new event in the 1984 Olympics. In this event groups of swimmers perform dancelike patterns in the water.

Water polo is an exciting team game in the water. The seven members of each team try to score points by throwing the ball into the other team's goal. Only one hand can be used to touch and throw the ball at any time. Water polo is a fast and exciting game.

Munich, 1972:
Mike Burton
(U.S.) wins
1,500-meter
freestyle
swimming.

Munich, 1972:
Canadians play
Yugoslavs in
water polo.

Boating and Canoeing

Boat and canoe races are another exciting part of the Olympics. Sailboats race with the wind around courses set in the water. Each boat goes as close as it can to markers in the water. If the boat touches the marker the boat is out of the race. Sailboats may be big or small. And they may have crews of one person or many people.

Rowing races are usually held on rivers and lakes. The rowers sit in narrow boats called shells, or skulls. They pull their oars through the water. When there is more than one rower, everyone must row together as a team. Sometimes one person faces the rowers and calls out the speed and directions. He is called a coxswain.

Canoe races are for one or two people. Canoers use paddles to move their canoes through the water.

Opposite: Munich, 1972: Kayak singles
Left: Munich, 1972: The canoe slalom

BALL SPORTS

Many kinds of ball games are played all over the world. At the Olympics there are competitions in basketball, field hockey, soccer, team handball, and volleyball. By 1988 tennis and table tennis will be part of the Olympics as well.

Basketball

Basketball is a game for two teams. There are five players on each team. A team scores points by throwing the ball through one of the baskets. They also try to prevent the other team from making baskets at the other end of the basketball court.

Munich, 1972: Olympic basketball

Munich, 1972: Women's volleyball

Volleyball

Volleyball is a game for two teams. There are six players on each team. The teams stand on a court divided by a high net. They hit the ball back and forth. Each team tries to keep the ball from hitting the ground on its own side. They must not hit the ball out of bounds or into the net. Both men's and women's teams play volleyball in the Olympics.

Munich, 1972: Olympic soccer

Soccer

The game that is called soccer in the United States is called football in most parts of the world. Except for the goalkeeper, the players move the ball with their feet. There are eleven people on each soccer team. They try to kick the ball into the goal defended by the other team. They also try to prevent the other team from kicking the ball into their goal.

Field Hockey

Field hockey is a game that is something like soccer. Both are played on a large field about the same size as an American football field. The field has a goal at each end. As in soccer, two eleven-man teams try to put the ball into the other team's goal. In field hockey, however, the ball is hit with a stick instead of kicked.

Team handball

Team handball is a combination of soccer, basketball, and field hockey. The seven players use a ball about 6 inches (15 cm) wide. They throw it into goals at either end of the handball court.

Munich, 1972: Field hockey

GYMNASTICS

One of the most popular sports to watch at the Olympics is gymnastics. With what looks like no effort, the gymnasts leap, twirl, and spin through the air. But every move needs perfect balance and muscle control.

Like divers, gymnasts are judged for their performances. Each judge gives the performance a score from one to ten. Ten is the best. Then all the judges' scores are averaged for the final score. In 1976 Nadia Comaneci from Rumania amazed everyone by getting a final score of ten in the competition on the uneven parallel bars. Nadia then amazed people even more when she got six more perfect scores.

Most gymnastic events are for individuals. But each country also sponsors a gymnastic team.

Montreal, 1976:
Nadia Comaneci
of Rumania
performs a flip on
the balance beam.

Women compete in four gymnastic events in the Olympics. They are the balance beam, floor exercises, the vaulting horse, and the uneven parallel bars. Each gymnast gets a score in each event. She also gets an overall score.

The balance beam is a few feet off the ground. It is made of wood and is about 4 inches (10 cm) wide and 16 feet (4.8 m) long. The gymnast jumps, steps, balances, and does somersaults on the beam.

The uneven bars are two bars about 3 feet (.9 m) away from each other. One bar is higher than the other. The gymnasts swing and twirl around the bars.

In the floor exercises the gymnasts tumble, jump, and balance on a floor mat. For women's competitions this is done to music. In many ways the floor exercises are like a modern dance.

Montreal, 1976:
Olga Korbut of
the U.S.S.R. frozen
in midair between
the uneven bars

The vaulting horse is a padded "horse." The gymnasts use it to perform jumps, handsprings, and cartwheels. Women go over the vaulting horse crosswise. Men go over it lengthwise.

Gymnastic competitions for men include the vaulting horse, the side horse, parallel bars, the high bar, and hanging rings.

The side horse is just like the vaulting horse except that it has two handles. Sometimes it is called the pommel horse.

The parallel bars are used for swinging and balancing. The two wooden bars are 1½ feet (.45 m) apart and about 5 feet (1.5 m) off the floor. In the high bar event the men swing and balance on a single bar set 8 feet (2.4 m) off the floor.

The hanging rings are like the rings used by circus performers. Gymnasts hold the rings with their hands and swing and turn. The rings may be held still or they may swing.

Moscow, 1980:
Alexander Dityatin
(U.S.S.R.) wins
a gold medal.

Montreal, 1976:
An Olympic boxing match

SPORTS OF
STRENGTH AND DEFENSE

Boxing

Boxing is an ancient sport in which two people hit each other with their fists. Modern boxers cover their fists with padded leather gloves. This helps to keep them from getting hurt.

Boxers are divided into groups by their weight. Boxers in the lightest group are called mini-flyweights. They weigh under 108 pounds (49 kg). Boxers in the heaviest group are called heavyweights. They weigh more than 175 (79.2 kg) pounds. A boxer can fight only in his own or in a heavier weight group.

Each fight is divided into parts called rounds. Each round lasts two or three minutes. Usually there are ten rounds in a fight.

A boxer can win in three ways. He can knock the other boxer down for ten seconds. When one boxer is taking a beating the referee can stop the fight. This is called a technical knockout, or a TKO. Each round is also scored. The referee and judges can use the scores to decide which fighter won the most rounds.

*Munich, 1972:
An Olympic
wrestling bout*

Wrestling

Like boxing, wrestling is an ancient sport for two men.
Using his hands and his body, each wrestler tries to
hold, or pin, the other to the ground. Wrestlers get
points for pinning the other, for keeping the other
under his control, and for escaping holds.

Judo

The Japanese sport of judo has been part of the
Olympics since 1972. Each judo fighter tries to throw
the other to the ground or to get him or her in a
choking hold.

The secret of judo is to try to turn the opponent's strength against him or her. Certain judo moves can be used in self-defense.

Each judo player wears a loose shirt and pants. This costume is called a "gi." The color of the player's belt shows his or her level. Beginners wear white belts. The most advanced players wear black.

Montreal, 1976: Men's judo lightweight finals

Fencing

Fighting with swords is called fencing. Three kinds of swords are used in the Olympics. They are the foil, the épée, and the saber. The foil is about 32 inches (80 cm) long and has four sides. The épée is heavier than a foil and has a three-sided blade. Both the foil and the épée have a guard on the tip. The saber has a blunt tip but a sharp blade.

A fencer scores points by touching the other player with the tip of his or her sword. Then he or she says "touché!" Today's swords also give an electric signal when the tip is touched. This helps in scoring.

Montreal, 1976: Épée individual fencing

Montreal, 1976: Middle heavyweight weightlifting

Weightlifting

Weightlifting is a sport that tests strength. Each weightlifter must raise a weighted bar above his head. If he raises it first to his chest and then over his head, it is called the "clean and jerk." If the weight is lifted over the head right away it is called a "snatch."

Like boxers, weightlifters are divided into groups according to body weight. The strongest weightlifters can lift over 500 pounds (226.5 kg)!

Montreal, 1976:
Olympic archery

SHOOTING SPORTS

Archery

Archery is the sport of shooting arrows with a bow. From 30 to 90 meters (100 to 300 feet) away the players shoot at a target. They score the most points for hitting the center of the target, or the bull's-eye.

Shooting

Both pistols and rifles are used for Olympic shooting events. People shoot at still targets and at moving objects.

RIDING SPORTS

Equestrian
Equestrian events are competitions for riders on horses. The horses must be able to jump, turn, balance, and trot at signals from their riders. Riders can compete as teams or individuals.

Cycling
Except for the 1904 games, bicycle races have always been part of the modern Olympics. Some of the races are held on an indoor track called a velodrome. Others are held outdoors on roads. Races are held for both teams and individuals.

Mexico City, 1968: The Italian cycling team

MODERN PENTATHLON

This Olympic event tests a person's skill at five different sports. It is both an individual and a team event. The contestants must ride a horse over an 800-meter (900-yard) course. They must fence with an épée. They must shoot a pistol at a target 25 meters (82 feet) away. They must swim 300 meters (330 yards). And they must run a 4,000-meter (4,400-yard) race. Like the decathlon and track-and-field pentathlon, this is a test of an all-around athlete.

When the last event of the Summer Olympics is over, the lighted torch is put out. The thousands of people who watched and took part in the Olympics then go home. Many of the athletes will work to do even better in the next Olympics four years later.

It is an honor to win a medal or a diploma at the Olympic Games. It is a reward for many hours of training and practice. But even for the athletes who do not win, it is a great experience to be in the Olympics. It gives them the chance to compete against the best in their field. For everyone it is a chance to travel and to make friends from all over the world.

Index

s 6/13 Lm P/12 4 crc 3 lib

S-2/14 LU-8/12 4 circs 3 libs